# 12 STORIES ABOUT HELPING CHILDREN

by Marne Ventura

STORY LIBRARY
MORE TO EXPLORE

www.12StoryLibrary.com



12-Story Library is an imprint of Bookstaves.

Photographs ©: Happy Together/Shutterstock.com, cover, 1; tablenc.org, 4; Susan Pierson/CC4.0, 4; Africa Studio/Shutterstock.com, 5; Library of Congress, 6; Everett Historical/Shutterstock.com, 7; War Child/PD, 8; Ajdin Kamber/Shutterstock.com, 8; kafeinkolik/Shutterstock.com, 9; Patty Henek/YouTube, 10; Patty Henek/YouTube, 11; crazyalcayne/YouTube, 12; Kevin Douglas/YouTube, 13; PD, 14; Rena Schild/Shutterstock.com, 14; DoSomething.org/YouTube, 15; Monkey Business Images/Shutterstock.com, 16; Lili Aini/Shutterstock.com, 17; Michal Kalasek/Shutterstock.com, 18; LowellMilkenCtr/YouTube, 18; LowellMilkenCtr/YouTube, 19; Anjo Kan/Shutterstock.com, 20; Jevanto Productions/Shutterstock.com, 20; Primus Inter Pares/CC2.0, 21; Claudio Stocco/Shutterstock.com, 22; rmeeba/Shutterstock.com, 23; Kim Peterson/YouTube, 24; PD, 24; DNF Style/Shutterstock.com, 25; Ken Wolter/Shutterstock.com, 26; s_bukley/Shutterstock.com, 26; Evan Vucci/Associated Press, 27; Fevziie/Shutterstock.com, 28; Rawpixel.com/Shutterstock.com, 29

**ISBN**
9781632357427 (hardcover)
9781632358516 (paperback)
9781645820277 (ebook)

**Library of Congress Control Number: 2019938656**

Printed in the United States of America
October 2019

## About the Cover

A tutor helps a student with reading.

Access free, up-to-date content on this topic plus a full digital version of this book. Scan the QR code on page 31 or use your school's login at 12StoryLibrary.com.

# Table of Contents

1

# TABLE: Feeding Hungry Children

Joy MacVane lives in Chapel Hill, North Carolina. Students at the University of North Carolina (UNC) walk by her house on their way to school. In 2006, she started baking cookies to share with them. She and a dozen students became friends. They began volunteering together at a homeless shelter.

MacVane and her team learned that almost a third of local children were not getting enough to eat. These children were on the school lunch program. They were given meals on school days, but on weekends, many went hungry.

In 2007, MacVane and her team created TABLE. Their mission is to provide healthy emergency food aid to hungry children. Students and community members donate food, money, and time. They pack up and deliver food to local schools at the end of each week. Children can bring the food home to eat over the weekend. Some children are at risk for hunger during the summer. TABLE delivers food to community centers and schools for pick-up.

SnackChef is TABLE's after-school program. Volunteers teach children how to make snacks. The goal is to expose children to healthy foods. They encourage the children to try new fruits and vegetables and learn about nutrition.

TABLE needs about 100 student volunteers every week to help deliver healthy food to kids.

**700+**

**Number of children TABLE fed every week in 2018**

- In 2014, TABLE fed 300 elementary schoolchildren.
- The program was expanded to include preschoolers and middle schoolers.
- In 2017, TABLE moved to a larger space so they could feed more children.

## CHILD HUNGER

Over 12 million children in the United States live in households without enough food for everyone to live a healthy life. Children get smaller portions than they need. Parents can't afford safe, nutritious foods. This is called "food insecurity." Federal nutrition programs such as SNAP and WIC help families buy food.

# 2

# Mother Jones: Child Labor Champion

Mother Jones circa 1910.

Mother Jones fought for the rights of working children. Not quite five feet (1.5 m) tall, she looked like a mild-mannered grandmother. But one US district attorney called her "the most dangerous woman in America."

She was born Mary Harris in Ireland between 1830 and 1844. When she was 10 years old, her family immigrated to North America to escape hunger and poverty. She married and had a family.

In 1867, a yellow fever epidemic killed her husband and four children.

The Industrial Revolution (1850–1940) in America brought big changes. Poor children worked in factories and coal mines. The work was dangerous, the hours long, the pay low. Workers formed groups called unions to fight for

**1916**

**Year when the US Congress passed the Keating-Owen Child Labor Act**

- Mother Jones helped bring the act to Congress.
- It called for an eight-hour workday and a minimum age of 14 for factory workers.
- The act was ruled unconstitutional in 1918.

better conditions. Jones became an advocate for labor unions. The union men called her "Mother" because she was a strong, effective leader.

Sixteen thousand children worked in silk factories in Philadelphia. The union wanted the work week to be cut from 60 to 55 hours. In 1903, Jones led a group of child workers and their parents in a march from Philadelphia to New York City. Thousands of people came out to see them. To show wealthy New Yorkers the plight of the children, Jones marched them to President Theodore Roosevelt's summer home on Long Island.

## CHILD LABOR LAWS

In 1938, the US Labor Department passed the Fair Labor Standards Act. It ensures that when young people work, the work is safe. It limits the number of hours school-age youth can work. For example, 14- or 15-year-olds cannot work more than three hours on a school day.

Young children working in a thread spinning factory in 1912.

# 3

# War Child: Helping Children Cope with Trauma

In 1993, two British filmmakers were working in war-torn Bosnia. David Wilson and Bill Leeson were shocked to see the hardships of children in war zones. They started War Child. They set up a bakery on wheels in Mostar, Bosnia. They baked tens of thousands of loaves of bread per day. They fed 15,000 people each week.

Today War Child has branches in Australia, Canada, Holland, Sweden, and the United States. Their mission is to protect, educate, and stand up for the rights of children caught up in war. War Child wants children to grow up free from fear and violence. They help get children out of war zones. When schools are destroyed, they set up learning centers. They counsel families to help them cope with the trauma of war. They help older children prepare for careers. They give legal aid to families.

Zariya and her family lived on a farm in Mosul, Iraq. For two years, ISIS,

War Child helps children get out of war zones so they can feel safe and go to school.

a militant group, controlled the city. Eight-year-old Zariya was scared of the soldiers. She wasn't allowed to go out. Her friends moved away. It was too dangerous to go to school. The fighting was all around.

One day a bomb destroyed Zariya's house. She was buried in rubble. It took her family 15 minutes to find her. Without a home, the family moved to a refugee camp. Zariya was sad and afraid. A War Child worker befriended her. The worker helped her feel more comfortable. Zariya started going to the school set up by War Child.

**9**

**Number of countries where War Child works**

- Some of the countries are Afghanistan, Iraq, Syria, and Yemen.
- 41,000 children from Mosul attended War Child's temporary schools.
- In 2016, 3,162 children were supported by War Child.

# 4

# LemonAid: Kids Helping Kids

On September 11, 2001, Islamic terrorists hijacked four planes. They caused the deaths of 3,000 people in the United States. A group of moms in a neighborhood near Chicago, Illinois, wanted to do something positive on the first anniversary of 9/11. They wanted their kids to participate. They set up a lemonade stand on Bonnie Brae Street in the town of River Forest.

They called their stand LemonAid. The children made and sold drinks and baked goods. By the end of the afternoon, they had raised $400. They gave the money to a local group that helps at-risk children. The following year, the stand raised $900 for a food bank.

Each year, the LemonAid stand grows. Local businesses set up stands. They give out free goodies. Musicians play. The local fire and police departments send representatives. In 2017, 3,000 people came. The town had to close the street.

Teens and younger children who live on Bonnie Brae help organize the event. They make a list of local groups that help children. The neighbors vote for one or two. The kids get the voting information to everyone on the block. They tally the votes and hold meetings to plan the event. They tell the local newspaper, radio, and TV stations about LemonAid.

## $250,000

**Total funds raised by LemonAid between 2002 and 2017**

- The group's mission is to turn lemonADE into lemonAID.
- The event has grown from one table to a whole, closed-off block.
- Funds raised grew from $400 in 2002 to $36,000 in 2017.

## LEMONAID PLACE

The families who started the LemonAid event live on the same block of Bonnie Brae. The entire neighborhood has worked together on the event since 2002. The Village Board of River Forest wanted to recognize their good work. In 2011, they voted to name the block LemonAid Place.

LemonAid kids making a donation to a local community center.

5

# Kevin Gatlin: Fun Hospital Sheets

Kevin Gatlin demonstrates the games that can be played on the sheets he developed.

Kevin Gatlin is a father in Charlotte, North Carolina. In 2014, he went to visit a friend's child in the hospital. Driving home, he felt sad for the child. Being stuck in bed all day is boring. Gatlin thought about his two sons. Their bedroom was too small for a desk or table. They often sat on their beds to play board games or do homework.

Gatlin had an idea. He would make fun, colorful sheets for children. He would print games like checkers or tic-tac-toe right on the fabric. It would give children on bed rest something to do. Gatlin spent two years designing the sheets. He got help from his wife, his mother (a teacher), and a family doctor.

By 2019, Gatlin's sheets were used in 25 children's hospitals. The pillows are printed with story starters. The sheets have giant board games, messages such as "I am strong," and colorful shapes. There are mazes and word games.

Gatlin hopes his sheets will give children in hospitals an alternative to watching TV or using a tablet. He hopes children will make friends with other patients and hospital staff.

## 50

**Number of games printed on Kevin Gatlin's sheets**

- Game pieces can be coins or paper cutouts.
- Gatlin sold two cars and some furniture to raise money for his business.
- He teamed up with other African American businesses to donate hundreds of sheets to the University of North Carolina Children's Hospital.

## THINK ABOUT IT

How is playing checkers or word games different than watching a TV show or playing a videogame? What are the pros and cons of each?

# 6 DoSomething.org: A Global Movement for Good

DoSomething.org is a website for social change. Young people go there to learn about ways to transform their communities. There are ideas here for every US area code and 131 countries around the world.

Users sign up as members. Members join campaigns. Each campaign is about a problem. Members are given instructions for how to help solve it. Young people can do good deeds without money, a car, or help from a parent or teacher. They can post a photo of themselves doing good deeds. They can get their friends to join in. The good deeds are easy and fun.

One campaign is called Huddle Against Hunger. The problem: 12 million young people in the United States don't get enough food. Members are given a list of food items to donate. They get information on how to find food centers in their area.

Andrew Shue, founder.

DO SOMETHING .ORG

DoSomething.org was started by American actor Andrew Shue and his friend Michael Sanchez. Shue has a history of helping others. In high school, he started a student group to help the elderly. After college, he and Sanchez spent a year in Africa teaching school. In 1993, Shue and Sanchez created DoSomething.org to give young people a way to make the world a better place.

**1,021,041**

**Pairs of jeans donated in one year to homeless youth**

- The jeans were donated through DoSomething.org's Teens for Jeans campaign.
- Bake Sale for Babies raised over $20,000 for babies in Syria.
- Birthday Mail made and mailed 290,000 cards to youth in homeless shelters.

## EMOJI OF COLOR

One DoSomething.org campaign helped fix a problem with Apple's emoji collection. Out of 800 emojis, only two showed people of color. Members told Apple that people of color need to be represented. They tweeted pictures of themselves to Tim Cook, the head of the company. It worked. The next operating system had a diverse set of emojis.

7

# Fayette County and New Mexico: Stopping School Lunch Shaming

In 2016, the National School Lunch Program served over 30.4 million children in the United States. The federal government pays for free or low-cost meals for children from low-income families. Three-fourths of US schools are owed money by families on the low-cost meal program.

In some of those schools, lunch shaming is a problem. Children whose parents owe money are singled out. Some schools serve them cheaper, smaller meals. Sometimes children's hands are stamped with a message for their parents. Some children are not given any food. These acts leave children hungry and embarrassed.

In Cornersville, Indiana, one in four children live in poverty. More than 60 percent qualify for free- or low-price lunch at school. For some of the children, that's all the food they get. Fayette County Schools wants these children to focus on schoolwork, not hunger. They don't want them to feel

Fayette County Schools offers all children a free breakfast to eat in the classroom.

ashamed because their parents can't pay. So every school in the district offers every child a free breakfast. It doesn't matter whether they can pay or not. Students eat in the classroom so it doesn't take away from class time. High schools offer a "second chance breakfast" for teens who get hungry later.

In 2017, New Mexico became the first state to outlaw school shaming. The Hunger-Free Students' Bill of Rights directs schools to talk to parents, not children, about unpaid bills. Whether a bill is paid or not, a student must be given a healthy meal.

**345,000**

**Number of free breakfasts served in Fayette County Schools in 2016**

- In 2018, California, Hawaii, Oregon, and Texas passed laws to stop school lunch shaming.
- Several other states are working on passing such laws.
- President Harry Truman first signed the National School Lunch Act in 1946.

# 8

# Sir Nicholas Winton: Humble Hero

Nicholas Winton in 2011 (right) and during the war.

On the eve of World War II (1939–1945), Nicholas Winton saved the lives of hundreds of children. Most were Jewish. Without his help, they would have been sent to Nazi concentration camps.

Winton was born in London in 1909. In 1938, he visited friends in Prague, Czechoslovakia. He was touched by the plight of the Jewish refugees who fled Nazi Germany. Now it seemed that Hitler would invade Czechoslovakia. Jewish families in Prague were frantic to get their children out of the country. The parents weren't allowed to leave. But they would send their children away if it meant saving their lives.

Winton gathered information on more than 900 children. He found foster homes in England for all of them. He raised money and arranged for trains. He forged papers and bribed officials. Everything he did was very dangerous. Nazi agents were watching him. Finally, in March 1939, the first train carried children out of Prague. Over the next few months, six more trains followed. On September 1, 1939, Hitler invaded Poland and the borders were closed. No more trains could get through.

Winton saved many children. But he never talked about it afterward. Fifty years later, his wife found a scrapbook in the attic. It told the story of what Winton had done. She gave the scrapbook to a historian. Winton appeared on a British TV show and met many of the people he had saved. They called themselves "Winton's Children." In 1998, Winton was made a Member of the Order of the British Empire. He was knighted by Queen Elizabeth II in 2003.

**669**
**Number of children Nicholas Winton saved**

- Winton became a Royal Air Force officer in the war.
- He later worked to help elderly people.
- Sir Nicholas Winton died on July 1, 2015. He was 106 years old.

Some of the 669 children Winton saved.

# 9 Save the Children: Helping Kids in Crisis

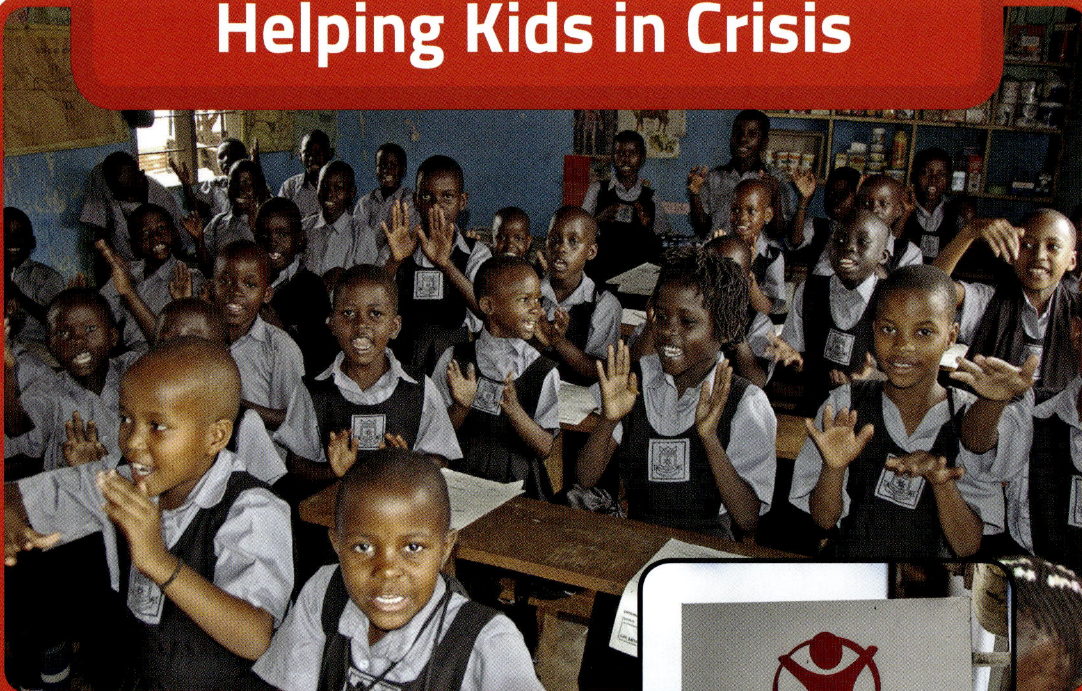

Save the Children has served at-risk children for 100 years. A federation of national groups in countries around the world, Save the Children helps children in poverty get an education. The groups fight for laws to protect children. They give out supplies after natural disasters. They set up safe play spaces in shelters. They help families bounce back after a crisis. They provide relief in war-torn areas.

Eglantyne Jebb founded the first Save the Children in London in 1919. Jebb was a wealthy, educated British woman. After World War I (1914–1918), children in Germany and Austria were starving. Save the Children raised money to help them. Today they help children and families around the world.

## THINK ABOUT IT

Do you agree that a good education is the way to help children escape poverty? Give two or three reasons for your answer.

**134 million**

**Children helped by Save the Children in 2018**

- Save the Children works in 120 countries around the world.
- Through Save the Children, people can sign up to sponsor an individual child.
- Save the Children says that while children are 20 percent of our population, they are 100 percent of our future.

Save the Children USA was formed in 1932 to help children during the Great Depression. Today they help children in poverty areas. They set up Early Childhood Education and Head Start programs. Their goal is to help children get out of poverty by getting a good education. Save the Children also shows up after natural disasters such as hurricanes.

Jebb wrote a list of children's rights in 1923. It became the basis of the Declaration of the Rights of the Child, which was adopted by the United Nations in 1959. Children's rights include life, protection, food, education, and health care.

A Save the Children worker helps a child suffering from malnutrition.

10

# Doctors Medical Center: Easing Children's Fears

Doctors and nurses at the Doctors Medical Center in Modesto, California, want to make it easier for children who need surgery. Normally a child going into surgery is put into a bed. The child has to sit and wait quietly. When it's finally time for the operation, hospital staff members wheel the bed down the hall. The child and parents have to say goodbye. It's a nerve-wracking ordeal for both the child and the parents.

Clowns dressed as doctors help children take their mind off surgery.

Hospitals are looking for ways to ease children's fears. Sometimes staff members show movies. They play games with the children. They bring in clowns dressed as doctors to make the children laugh.

Kimberly Martinez is a pre-op nurse at Doctors Medical. She suggested the hospital let

children drive a toy car into the operating room. The excitement of driving a car takes the child's mind off the surgery. Instead of feeling sad about being separated from their parents, the child is distracted by a fun experience. When the parents see their child having fun, it's easier for them to relax, too.

The hospital bought a black Mercedes mini car. One of the hospital workers donated a pink VW Beetle. Both mini-cars have a stereo with preloaded music and an MP3 player. They have working headlights, taillights, and dashboard lights.

## 2–7

**Ages of children who use the hospital mini-cars**

- The child can actually operate the car.
- Parents can use a remote control to help younger children drive.
- The cars have working doors, a seatbelt, and a horn.

## THINK ABOUT IT

Imagine a younger friend or sibling needs surgery. What ideas do you have for ways to calm their fears? How would you help them?

11

# Andrew Bridge: Fighting for Foster Care Rights

Andrew Bridge overcame a traumatic childhood to become a lawyer and best-selling author. He has devoted his career to making life better for children in foster care. Bridge's young mother was mentally ill. She was poor, and her husband abandoned her. Bridge loved his mother and wanted to be with her. When he was seven, Los Angeles police took him away from his mother and put him in an orphanage. Then he was placed in a foster home in Southern California. The family treated Bridge badly, but social workers left him there for 11 years.

Only two percent of the 500,000 children in foster care in the United States get a college degree. They are more likely to end up homeless or in prison. Bridge beat the odds. He worked hard in high school. He got a scholarship to Wesleyan University in Connecticut. He graduated from Harvard Law School. At that point, he could have pursued

Andrew Bridge's book, *Hope's Boy*, was a *New York Times* Bestseller.

## 2008

**Year when Andrew Bridge's life story, *Hope's Boy*, was published**

- Bridge believes welfare agencies should work harder to keep troubled families together.
- He works to help young single parents keep their children.
- He helped start a Los Angeles college preparatory school for children in foster care.

## FOSTER CARE FACTS

About 443,000 children are in foster care in the United States every day. Most stay in foster care for two years. The average age of kids entering care is eight. In 2017, a third of all children going into foster care were young people of color.

a career as a highly paid corporate lawyer. Instead, he chose to fight for children in foster care.

Bridge became head of the California-based Alliance for Children's Rights. He increased the free legal services available to children in foster care. He helped speed up the process for foster parents to adopt children. He led efforts to help at-risk children get a better education.

# 12 Boys & Girls Clubs: Helping Kids Succeed

In 1860, three women in Hartford, Connecticut, started a club for street kids. Mary Goodwin, Alice Goodwin, and Elizabeth Hammersley wanted the boys to have a positive alternative. They believed this would help them grow up to be good citizens. The women invited the boys into their homes. They played games and read with them. They made the boys feel cared for. The club grew.

By 1931, more clubs had formed across the United States. They joined together as Boys Clubs of America. In 1990, they became Boys & Girls Clubs of America. Clubs have programs for sports, recreation, and education. They help kids learn about the arts, health, wellness, and careers. They offer character education and leadership training.

Jennifer Lopez and Denzel Washington with children from the Boys & Girls Club in Los Angeles, CA.

First Lady Michelle Obama works on a service project with kids at the Boys & Girls Club in Washington, DC.

## 4.2 million

**Number of boys and girls served by the Boys & Girls Clubs of America**

- 97 percent of Club teens plan to graduate from high school.
- 88 percent plan to complete college or vocational school.
- 52 percent of 12th grade Club members plan on a STEM career, compared with 27 percent nationally. STEM stands for science, technology, engineering, and math.

## BOYS & GIRLS CLUBS ALUMNI HALL OF FAME

Each year, the Boys & Girls Clubs honor a group of men and women who began their future within Club walls and have gone on to great things. The 2019 honorees included a US Army Brigade Commander, a World Wrestling Entertainment Women's Champion, and an NFL Hall of Famer.

The clubs have helped many children become successful adults. Denzel Washington is an award-winning actor. He gives the Mount Vernon, Virginia, club credit for being a good influence on him. Many of his friends from the same neighborhood ended up in prison. Jennifer Lopez is an actress, singer, and dancer. She was one of the first members of the Kips Bay, New York, Boys & Girls Club Performing Arts Program.

## Ways You Can Help

- Every second Saturday in May, letter carriers across the United States collect food for the hungry. Just place a box or can of nonperishable food next to your mailbox.
- Gather toys and books you no longer use. Donate them to a local homeless shelter.
- Clip coupons for food your parents buy. Ask if they will donate the money saved to a good cause.
- Clean out your closet and donate clothes that no longer fit to a shelter or charity.
- Be kind to others. If a classmate needs help, offer to help. If they are alone, invite them to join you and your friends.
- If your school has a program, offer to tutor younger students who need help.
- Pack an extra sandwich in your lunch. Offer it to a classmate who doesn't have a lunch.

- When new students come to your school, be friendly. Show them around. Make them feel welcome.
- Get together with a group of friends. Share ideas for helping kids in your community. Pick one and get started.

# Glossary

**advocate**
Someone who argues for or supports a group or a cause.

**at-risk child**
A child who is likely to have trouble in school and in life.

**charity**
A group that helps people in need.

**concentration camp**
A place where large numbers of people are imprisoned, often for political reasons, in terrible conditions.

**donate**
To give money, food, clothing, books, time, or something else you have to help others.

**federation**
A group of organizations that have joined together to make a large organization.

**foster**
To act as a parent for a child in need.

**labor**
Work done for pay.

**nutrition**
The act of eating healthy food.

**refugee**
A person who flees home because of war or persecution.

**trauma**
Physical or mental stress.

**volunteer**
A person who works without pay in order to help.

**welfare**
A government program to help people in need.

# Read More

Lopez, Elizabeth Anderson. *Fantastic Kids: Helping Others.* Huntington Beach, CA: Teacher Created Materials, 2017.

Dean, Amie. *Your Happy Heart: How Helping Others Helps You, Too.* Chattanooga, TN: National Center for Youth Issues, 2019.

Roy, Jennifer. *Jars of Hope: How One Woman Helped Save 2,500 Children During the Holocaust.* North Mankato, MN: Capstone Publishers, 2016.

# Index



## About the Author

Marne Ventura has written 100 books for children. A former elementary school teacher, she holds a master's degree in education from the University of California. Marne and her husband live on the central coast of California.